Development Centre Studies

Can we still Achieve the Millennium Development Goals?

FROM COSTS TO POLICIES

Jean-Philippe Stijns, Christopher Garroway,
Vararat Atisophon, Jesus Bueren, Gregory De Paepe
and Carlos Sanchez

OECD dev
DEVELOPMENT CENTRE

The opinions expressed and arguments employed in this publication do not necessarily reflect those of the OECD, its Development Centre or of the governments of their member countries.

This document and any map included herein are without prejudice to the status of or sovereignty over any territory, to the delimitation of international frontiers and boundaries and to the name of any territory, city or area.

Please cite this publication as:
OECD (2012), *Can we still Achieve the Millennium Development Goals?: From Costs to Policies,*
Development Centre Studies, OECD Publishing.
http://dx.doi.org/10.1787/9789264173248-en

ISBN 978-92-64-17323-1 (print)
ISBN 978-92-64-17324-8 (PDF)

Series: Development Centre Studies
ISSN 1563-4302 (print)
ISSN 1990-0295 (online)

Foreword

In 2000, the international community came together to agree upon the Millennium Development Goals (MDGs) and in so doing committed itself to working together to put an end to poverty, hunger, disease and lack of adequate shelter by 2015. Gender equality, education and environmental sustainability were to be promoted along with basic rights to health, education, safe drinking water and sanitation. To achieve these goals, the international community, including the OECD, agreed to build up a global partnership for development.

Twelve years later, hundreds of millions of people have moved out of extreme poverty and, in 2010, the world achieved the MDG of halving the number of poor people, mainly thanks to high growth in large countries such as Brazil, China and India. However, the challenges of fighting extreme poverty in all countries and of achieving the other MDGs remain. The ever-growing number of financing instruments and entities creates an increasingly complex architecture of development co-operation but, at the same time, allows a better mobilisation of untapped development resources, including the sharing of development knowledge across the world.

This study builds on OECD Development Centre Working Paper No. 306[1] and the Development Centre's long-standing work on development finance, fiscal policy for development, the rise of emerging countries and social cohesion. It endeavours to bring these results to a wide audience and to highlight their policy implications in the run-up to 2015 and beyond. The first aim is to revisit the cost estimations of the Millennium Development Goals to which development agencies contributed during the early 2000s. The second aim is to provide an assessment of developing countries' own capacity to fund additional development investment through domestic resources, taxes in particular, and external resources, such as FDI, remittances, private donations and aid.

Can We Still Achieve the Millennium Development Goals? From Costs to Policies is the result of a successful collaboration with the Bill and Melinda Gates Foundation. This study also conveys results from work done with the financial support of the French Ministry of Foreign and European Affairs. The project has also benefited from the intellectual input of the National Treasury of South Africa and of the South African office of the UN Development Programme as well as the members of the Centre's Development Finance Network.[2]

Notes

1. http://www.oecd.org/dataoecd/39/5/49301301.pdf
2. The Centre's Development Finance Network (DeFiNe) is a global network of think-tanks, research centres and academic institutions from developing, emerging and OECD countries, co-ordinated by the OECD Development Centre.

Acknowledgements

Can we still Achieve the Millennium Development Goals? From Costs to Policies is the result of a successful collaboration with the Bill and Melinda Gates Foundation. The authors wish to express their gratitude for the generous support of the Foundation as well as for its suggestions and comments. This study also conveys the results of work carried out with the financial support of the French Ministry of Foreign and European Affairs.

The study builds on OECD Development Centre Working Paper No. 306 by Vararat Atisophon, Jesus Bueren, Gregory De Paepe, Christopher Garroway de Coninck and Jean-Philippe Stijns. Many colleagues, including an anonymous reviewer chosen by the Bill and Melinda Gates Foundation, have provided us rich comments on the working paper. In particular, we thank Simon Scott (director of the Statistics Division of the OECD Development Co-operation Directorate), Helmut Reisen (director of research at the OECD Development Centre) and Mumukshu Patel (Global Development Programme of the Bill and Melinda Gates Foundation). We are indebted to the participants of the workshop on "The Costs of MDGs: Investing in Development by 2015 and Beyond" co-organised by the Development Centre in partnership with the South African Institute of International Affairs (SAIIA), the National Treasury of South Africa, and the South African office of the UN Development Programme in Pretoria on Monday 14 November 2011. Comments from Neil Cole, secretary general of CABRI, have been particularly helpful in taking our work forward.

Many experts have devoted their time to examining preliminary versions of this study and have provided comments and suggestions that have greatly contributed to enriching it. We would particularly like to thank David Batt and Karim Hussein (director and adviser of the OECD Africa Partnership Forum), Laurent Bossard (director of the Sahel and West Africa Club), Dr. Bruce Byiers (chief analyst of governance and trade at ECDPM), Dr. Homi Kharas (senior fellow and deputy director at the Brookings Institute), David Mc Nair (principal adviser for economic justice at Christian Aid), Dr. Ángel Melguizo (lead specialist at the Inter-American Development Bank) and Benedicte Vibe Christensen (independent public policy analyst).

We express thanks to our colleagues in the OECD Directorate for Development Co-operation (DCD), Dr. Hildegard Lingnau (senior policy advisor) for her advice, Fredrik Ericsson (statistics analyst) and Emily Bosch (policy analyst) for their many suggestions and very constructive criticism. We would also like to thank the representatives of the members of DeFINe think tanks that offered us their comments and suggestions at the annual meeting of their network on 27 March 2012, on the occasion of the opening of the week of the 50th anniversary of the Development Centre.

The authors are also grateful to their colleagues in the Centre and in particular Federico Bonaglia and Papa Amadou Sarr (respectively head of division and regional policy co-ordinator, Policy Dialogue Division), Henri-Bernard Solignac Lecomte and Jan Rieländer (respectively head of unit and economist, Europe, Africa and Middle East desk), Edouard Turkisch (policy analyst), Johannes Jütting and Juan de Laiglesia (respectively head of unit and economist, Poverty Reduction Unit).

This study would not have seen the day without the research and organisation assistance of Carlos Sánchez. We thank Timothy Witcher, Vanda Legrandgérard, and Anne-Lise Prigent for their help in editing this study, as well as Roger Hobby, Erik Cervin-Edin and Elodie Masson for communication and mobilisation of social networks.

All errors, gaps, and views expressed in this study remain the responsibility of the authors.

Table of contents

Figures

Boxes

Preface

The biggest gathering of world leaders ever assembled occurred in New York in 2000 to set eight broad, time-bound and quantified targets to beat extreme poverty, now known around the globe as the Millennium Development Goals (MDGs). With three years to go until the 2015 deadline to meet the MDGs, the question of how much it will cost and who will pay for one of the biggest campaigns ever launched by the international community is returning to everyone's lips.

This study assesses the financial cost of achieving the MDGs for the countries who have yet to reach them. It looks beyond aid and measures the ability of countries to achieve social development by themselves. The order of magnitude of the results implies that achieving the MDGs will be at least as much about policies and partnerships as it will be about financing. The conclusions of the first High Level Meeting of the OECD Development Centre's member countries reinforced this point, highlighting the importance of redefining national development strategies in a world in which the economic centre of gravity is shifting to the east and south.

Assessing progress on the MDGs is a useful framework for understanding, more broadly, how countries are progressing towards ensuring the sustainability of development. The underlying question is, how to upgrade the processes for evaluating and implementing policies over time, including managing public spending across all sectors and at all levels of government within a medium-term budget? The challenges must not be underestimated, but they are not insurmountable. An inclusive and in-depth dialogue between countries is key to improving policies. Developing countries have demonstrated their ability to innovate, and all countries have much to gain from discussing the successes and challenges of their development experience.

The OECD Development Centre is committed to actively sharing its 50 years of experience through publications, such as this study, and through inclusive policy dialogue. Our ambition is to contribute to the quality of public policies so as to support countries as they build thriving economies and cohesive societies, until 2015 and beyond.

Mario Pezzini
Director
OECD Development Centre
March 2012

Executive summary

This study contributes to the current debate on achieving the Millennium Development Goals (MDGs), their relevance and what can be done after 2015, by looking at estimates of the cost of reaching the goals in 2015. In particular, it sizes the additional resources needed in developing countries to attain the goals. The demand for cost estimates is growing as the 2015 deadline looms. Surprisingly, few recent works have sought to estimate and to find solutions for addressing the corresponding funding gaps.

Earlier contributions have focused on aid as the main source of new resources for attaining the goals without looking at the role of other sources such as domestic tax revenues, South-South co-operation, remittances from emigrants or private donations and capital. The additional cost of achieving the poverty, education and health goals has been approximated. An estimate of how increased revenues could be raised through improved taxation in developing countries – the public side of domestic resource mobilisation – is also provided. The numbers imply that the international community must broaden its notion of development co-operation beyond Official Development Assistance (ODA). There is a need to leverage the full spectrum of additional finance and prioritise political reforms in advanced and developing countries alike in order to help reach the level of social development equivalent to the MDGs.

The size of the challenge facing the development community

Several years after the 2008 International Conference in Doha on Financing for Development that took stock of the 2002 Monterrey consensus, financing development remains a major international challenge. Since the 1990s, the landscape of development finance has evolved with the emergence of new partners and modalities of financing. There has also been a welcome increase in public and private flows to developing countries. However, the severe impact of the global crisis has restricted the scope of such progress, raising new concerns.

While it is not an insurmountably high amount, the financial cost of achieving the Millennium goals is bigger than the figure that could be raised unless the full range of available development resources is properly mobilised and necessary policy reforms are pursued by all development partners. This study estimates this cost to be in the order of USD 120 billion. Around half of this amount is a "financing gap" concentrated in 20 low-income countries. The remaining half is needed for targeted transfers and spending in 79 other low- and middle-income countries. In comparison, this USD 120 billion shortfall is approximately double current country programmable aid, *i.e.* the portion of official development assistance most likely to help with meeting the MDGs. If aid alone could address the MDG challenge, it would have to triple its current level.

How the cost of the Millennium Development Goals is measured

The study uses two approaches: *i)* a bottom-up approach, which assesses the cost of directly addressing poverty, education and health goals through targeted transfers and expenditures; *ii)* a top-down approach, which measures the amount of development finance required to ensure that there is enough economic growth to meet the MDGs. The top-down approach measures are constructed as time-bound targets to be sustained until 2015, while the bottom-up approach assumes that targeted transfers and expenditure are always paid out each year and indefinitely. To generate the global cost, a choice is made, country-by-country, between the two approaches on a case-by-case basis, according to their relative cost. The characteristics of middle-income countries make the bottom-up approach the most cost-effective. For low-income countries the top-down approach has proven to be a better option. Please refer to Atisophon *et al.* (2011) for a detailed explanation of the methodology behind this study.

Figure 0.1.**Comparing the top-down *vs.* the bottom-up approach**

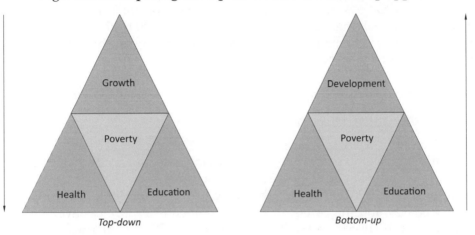

The trade-off between the top-down and bottom-up approach across high, medium and low-income countries illustrates and is explained by the structural characteristics of these countries. The countries with the greatest top-down "financing gap" are those where greater development finance – aid or private capital flows – would have the smallest effect on growth. This is characteristic of middle-income developing countries, which will fall short of reaching the MDG goals by 2015. These economies are essentially some of the most unequal and some of the least responsive to investment and aid. Conversely, in many low-income countries, it is less costly to boost – once and for all – the level of economic development through a significant rise in development finance than to pay, year-after-year, for the implicit costs of all the dimensions of poverty. Naturally, improvements in the productivity of investment – through reforming institutions and improving the business climate – can make a dramatic difference in the size of additional resources needed in middle-income countries. Reforming policies to make growth more inclusive and to improve the quality of public expenditure is obviously a crucial option. Efforts from development partners to increase aid effectiveness are also critical.

The cost of the fight against poverty

In comparison with figures from 1990, it is estimated that roughly 35 countries are expected to fall short of reaching the first goal of halving the number of people in poverty. Rapid poverty reduction in a few large countries will reduce global numbers to less than half of the 1990 level. Nevertheless, sub-Saharan Africa, Latin America and the Caribbean region are facing a substantial financial cost to halving poverty. Based on data from 2009, the annual cost of targeted transfers to lift half of the poor above the poverty line by 2015 (MDG 1) would be almost USD 5 billion.

The cost of education

Although overall school attendance has increased markedly over the past decade, it would still cost nearly USD 9 billion to achieve Universal Primary Education (UPE) by 2015 (MDG 2). Obviously, UPE is closely linked to promoting gender equality and the empowerment of women (MDG 3). On average, the countries that still need to reach the education target have to increase spending by slightly more than 7%, which should be achievable over time. The most challenging rate of increase in baseline expenditure is in sub-Saharan Africa, over 20%. Middle-income countries have the largest expenditure shortfall, nearly USD 8 billion in total. The Latin American and Caribbean regions require the highest increase in spending because of the high cost of education per student in the region.

The cost of health

Most of the extra health spending will be needed in sub-Saharan Africa and South Asia to cut child mortality by two thirds, reduce the maternal mortality ratio by three quarters and halt AIDS, malaria and other major diseases (MDGs 4-6). The highest costs are associated with health in low- and lower-middle countries, nearly USD 60 billion. In terms of regions in South Asia, USD 35 billion will be needed, and in sub-Saharan Africa, USD 20 billion.

Where the resources will come from

There is a high potential for middle-income countries to meet their needs by raising their own resources. The numbers confirm both the requisite role of ODA in a number of low-income countries and the important and growing role of other sources of development finance in all developing countries. Upper middle-income countries could mobilise enough domestic resources to meet the poverty, education and health goals. In contrast, ODA will remain a prime source of finance for many low-income countries. Using increased private capital is a real option for filling the financing gap for lower income countries, at least partially. But the volatility of these flows will have to be managed and there is a need to adjust national development strategies to optimise their spillovers in terms of social development. This also applies to the remittances of migrant workers that should contribute to investment more systematically, including in smaller businesses where it is missing. So if the needs of the poorest citizens in the poorest countries are to be met, all development sources – domestic taxes, private capital from traditional as well as emerging partners, private contributions, remittances and, of course aid – will play an important role.

The Millennium Development Goals

One – Eradicate Extreme Poverty and Hunger
Halve, between 1990 and 2015, the proportion of people who live on less than USD 1 a day, achieve full and productive employment for all and halve the proportion of people who suffer from hunger.

Two – Universal Primary Education
Ensure that, by 2015, children everywhere, boys and girls, complete primary schooling.

Three – Promote Gender Equality and Empower Women
Eliminate gender disparity in all levels of education by 2015.

Four – Reduce Child Mortality
Reduce the 1990 mortality rate among the under fives by two thirds by 2015.

Five – Improve Maternal Health
Reduce by three quarters the maternal mortality ratio and achieve universal access to reproductive health.

Six – Combat HIV/Aids, Malaria and Other Diseases
Have halted by 2015 and begun to reverse the spread of HIV/AIDS, with universal access to treatment for all those who need it. Halt and reverse the incidence of malaria and other major diseases.

Seven – Environmental Sustainability
Integrate the principles of sustainable development into country policies and programmes and reverse the loss of environmental resources. Reduce biodiversity loss and halve the proportion of the population without access to safe drinking water and basic sanitation.

Eight – Global Partnership
Develop an open, rule-based, predictable, non-discriminatory trading and financial system.

Chapter 1

The Millennium challenge

Abstract

Several years after the Monterrey Conference, progress on meeting the Millennium Development Goals (MDGs) has been uneven. Therefore, in the run up to the 2015 deadline, assessing the magnitude of the financing challenge is crucial. This study estimates the size of the corresponding financial costs, putting this in the context of both domestic and external development resources that are currently and could potentially become available. The estimated cost of attaining the goals is around USD 120 billion and is split evenly between low- and middle-income countries. The cost-effective option for low-income countries[1] is to close their financing gap so as to raise their growth rates in a sustainable manner. In the case of middle-income countries,[2] it is rather about targeted transfers and expenditure. From this perspective, it is extremely important to continue reforming tax administration and improving the quality of public expenditure.

Getting started

Aid budgets declined in the 1990s, but the MDGs helped to galvanise the international aid community towards committing itself to increasing resources for development co-operation in the 2000s. By the late 1990s, many developing countries had gone through shaky economic transitions, from socialist planning or debilitating financial crises – and in some cases both. Official Development Assistance (ODA) shrank after the end of the Cold War and many rich countries reduced their engagement in the developing world. The MDGs helped refocus the development community on measurable, achievable and time-bound goals. In particular, this invigorated the development co-operation efforts of OECD countries that are members of the Development Assistance Committee (DAC), re-igniting their engagement.

The most recent *Global Monitoring Report* (World Bank and IMF, 2011) shows that, overall, the number of people living on less than USD 1.25 a day will be cut by half even if progress is uneven across countries. The reports of the MDG Taskforce (2008-11) and the UNDP-UNCDF (2010) report warn that, while progress has been made on several fronts, important shortfalls persist. Seventeen countries in Africa will not halve extreme poverty by 2015. Furthermore, achieving the first Millennium objective of halving the proportion of people living on less than USD 1.25 a day is not necessarily a sign of conclusive success in the fight against poverty in its many dimensions. Indeed, moving from 40% to 20% of the population living in extreme poverty does not guarantee that the MDGs related to education and health are met, even though such change paradoxically represents very significant success in terms of structural transformation. The world is also still short of achieving gender parity in primary and secondary education, making sure all children complete primary education and providing access to safe drinking water. Moreover, global progress on child and maternal mortality is too slow.

Despite the consensus achieved by the Monterrey Conference on financing for development, financing remains a major international challenge. The development finance landscape has evolved with the emergence of new actors and new sources of financing. At the same time, efforts have been made to improve the efficiency of international financing. The Fourth High Level Forum on Aid Effectiveness in 2011 pointed to the need for broadening attention beyond aid effectiveness to effective development. The forum called for a new, inclusive and representative Global Partnership for Effective Development Co-operation.

Assessing the financial size of the outstanding challenges is crucial for advancing the international development debate and for achieving the MDGs. Table 1.1 surveys the estimates of MDG costs that have been prepared for all developing countries. These are highly focused on ODA while this survey shows that the scale of financing needed to achieve the goals requires development finance to look beyond ODA as its principal resource. Inasmuch as OECD member countries must respect their financial commitment and effective aid, it goes without saying that, in the lead up to 2015, the economic crisis is restricting the budgets and tightening the policies of these countries. Therefore, the MDGs will not be attainable by relying solely on ODA.

Table 1.1. **Previous global MDG cost estimates**

	Estimated additional annual cost (current USD billion)	Estimated additional annual cost (2009 USD billion)	Notes
United Nations (2001)	50	61	Estimates drawn from the Report of the High-Level Panel on Financing for Development, chaired by Ernesto Zedillo.
Devarajan *et al.* (2002)	54-62	63-72	First calculation based on financing gap for limited group of countries; second calculation based on estimated health, education, and environmental costs. The two are alternate calculations and should not be added up.
	35-75	41-87	
Millennium Project (2005)	72-135	82-152	Based on needed increases to ODA 2006-15, including increased donor commitments. Assumed USD 22.7 billion of USD 46.6 billion in ODA in 2002 went to MDGs based on four case studies of individual countries.

The study also shows that in the near future, ODA will remain essential for low-income countries in addition to other forms of development finance. While improved domestic tax collection makes a growing contribution to financing in all developing countries, in many low-income countries, domestic taxes cannot be expected to meet the MDG costs in the near future. Raising additional revenue takes time in low-income countries because of the strengthened institutional capacity required. While over time the objective is clearly for these countries to be aid-free, it will be critical to sequence policies properly. In these countries in particular, aid should definitely be maintained, ideally bolstered, and focused on strengthening domestic resource mobilisation.

Therefore, achieving the MDGs requires many conditions besides financing. Policy reforms are far more important than the mere question of financing and it is crucial not to assume that the most efficient response would necessarily be to increase development finance. Poor quality public expenditure remains a major hurdle for developing countries trying to meet the aspirations of their citizens. These countries are in need of good institutions that can design, implement and evaluate policies, especially for strong public expenditure management across all levels of government, good implementation capacity, and a medium-term fiscal policy that can ensure the sustainability of the MDGs.

The purpose of the study

As the 2015 deadline for attaining the MDGs approaches, albeit in a vastly different global economic and political climate to the one in which world leaders set the goals in 2000, the nature of development co-operation has changed. This change is due to the emergence of new poles of growth in the developing world as well as recession and increasing calls for fiscal austerity in rich countries. Partly out of necessity, sources for financing development have been diversified and include fast growing South-South co-operation, trade and investment flows. Although aid and development co-operation still play an important, catalytic role, there is a general recognition that aid alone cannot reduce poverty and foster development. A number of countries have also increased their capacity to collect tax revenue and to mobilise other domestic resources as forms of development finance. For instance, tax revenues are already ten times larger than ODA on the African continent even though this average conceals considerable country-to-country differences (AfDB, OECD and UNECA, 2010).

Development agencies contributed to estimates made in the early 2000s. Now it is time to update those figures. A fresh perspective on the capacity of countries to fund additional development investment on their own is needed. OECD Development Centre Working Paper No. 306 (Atisophon *et al.*, 2011) filled this void by providing new estimates about the cost of reaching the MDGs by 2015. This OECD Development Centre Study aims to share these results with a wider audience and to highlight the policy implications stemming from these estimates. Although we have reviewed basic aspects of the methodology used to estimate the cost of the MDGs throughout this study, please refer to the Working Paper and its appendices for technical details.

The purpose of this study is to offer an assessment of the size/scope of resources needed to achieve the MDGs in the developing world and to compare it with available domestic and external financial resources. The estimates are meant to help understand the financial magnitude of the problem that many countries face. To this effect, estimates are offered of how much achieving the MDGs would cost. Although it is not an insurmountably high amount, it is larger than the sum that could be raised from development co-operation alone, given the budgetary situation at the time of writing.

The figures discussed in the study are useful for drawing the big picture regarding the financial challenge associated with the MDGs and the resources and means that are available for achieving them. However, these figures should be interpreted as estimates and not be taken as precise indications, especially at the country level, of how much public expenditure would be required to achieve specific MDGs. There are many data and methodological challenges with modeling the cost of the goals. Devarajan *et al.* (2002) cautioned that prudence should be exerted while interpreting their own cost estimates, and that monetary inputs are not the only and certainly not the most important constraint limiting the attainment of the MDGs. Furthermore, in this respect, the situation can vary notably from one country to another. When estimating the amount of development finance required to reach the MDGs, transfers or government expenditure required for reaching poverty, education and health goals, it is important to acknowledge the fact that the link between inputs and outcomes is often uncertain and that absorption and delivery issues pose challenges in developing countries. Indeed, the importance of framing the debate in the larger framework of the quality of public policy and institutions is one key lesson learned in the exercise of estimating the cost of financing the MDGs.

The rest of this study is organised as follows:

- Chapter 1 provides an overall picture of how much it would cost to achieve the MDGs by 2015.

- Chapter 2 looks more specifically at the costs of combating poverty and improving health and education in developing countries.

- Chapter 3 reviews what means are available for the development community to achieve the goals in the coming years, both in terms of development finance that is currently available and the financial flows that can be relied upon for meeting the needs of developing countries.

- Chapter 4 summarises the broad policy options that it foresees for the international community in terms of the costs discussed in this study, bearing in mind the importance of keeping the momentum of the MDG alive in the run-up to 2015 and beyond.

The overall size of the challenge: the USD 120 billion question

Two separate sets of MDG cost estimates are used to provide the general scope of resources needed to achieve the Millennium goals. One set, referred to as "top-down" estimates is based on the premise that "a rising tide lifts all boats" and that sufficiently strong economic growth can spur sustainable development, particularly with respect to the forms of social development covered by the MDGs. The other set of estimates, referred to as "bottom-up", is founded on the simple argument that improving public spending on service delivery can lead to attaining the goals. In both cases, the implicit link assumed between financial flows and social outcomes is schematic since the connection between the estimated cost and the expected results is clearly uncertain. Nevertheless, these estimates serve the modest purpose for which they are intended. At a global level these calculations help provide a useful starting point for understanding the financial needs in countries and the nature of the reforms needed. On the one hand, as a corollary, policy reforms can and must play a key role in making growth more inclusive and more conducive to social development. On the other hand, they can also play a key role in improving the quality of public expenditure and the sustainability of its impact on growth.

The "top-down" financing gap measures are constructed as time-bound targets that are meant to raise domestic income to ensure that achieving the MDGs is self-sustaining. The "bottom-up" service delivery costs are conceived in a way that requires the corresponding transfers to be maintained beyond the 2015 deadline to ensure achieving the MDGs. The two sets of MDG costs cannot be added to each other for the same countries because otherwise, the cost of achieving the MDGs would be double-counted. The stated aim of the financing gap approach is to propel economies into a pattern of self-sustaining growth to escape the poverty trap, in its multi-dimensional forms, by covering its educational and health aspects, for instance. Financing gap measures, while imprecise, can be used to estimate the rough size of the temporary capital requirement needed to achieve sufficiently high growth rates to put the economy onto a self-sustaining growth path. Hence, the top-down approach assumes that growth can address all MDGs at once and on a sustainable basis. In contrast, a drop in expenditure linked to social development can lead to renewed poverty, a decline in child enrolment and a resurgence in child mortality, maternal mortality and pandemic diseases, ruining progress towards attaining the MDGs. The limits and merits of these two approaches are discussed in detail in Atisophon *et al.* (2011).

On an annual basis, the cost estimates for achieving the MDGs through bottom-up development service delivery is smaller than the estimates of the top-down capital requirement for achieving the growth needed to meet the MDGs. Figure 1.1 overleaf shows that the top-down financing gap calculations reflect a need for more than USD 280 billion in additional resources annually to achieve the MDGs. The bulk of these additional resources is estimated to be required in middle-income countries. Adopting a top-down approach for middle-income countries would require an annual USD 220 billion increase in development finance for these countries. This very high sum argues for a more direct, bottom-up approach for addressing the poverty, health and education goals of middle-income countries through transfers and expenditure. Such an approach reduces the cost of meeting MDGs in middle-income countries to less than USD 40 billion on an annual basis. The service delivery calculations lead to a global figure of tens of billions of dollars, while the financing gap is calculated to be in the order of hundreds of billions of dollars.

The fundamental reason why the top-down approach is systematically more expensive on an annual basis than the bottom-up approach is its assumption that the distribution of income is left unchanged. Indeed, it requires the income of the entire population to be lifted to decrease the proportion of the population living in absolute poverty. However, by implicitly assuming that a constant share of GDP is spent on health and education, the top-down approach is supposed to address all the MDGs in a sustainable manner and not only the goal of halving extreme poverty (MDG 1). In contrast, the bottom-up approach directly addresses the MDGs related to poverty, education and health at a constant level of economic development. The bottom-up approach is thus more cost-effective. However, it implies that transfers and expenditures are maintained indefinitely. The bottom-up approach is therefore more cost-effective. However, it assumes the continuation of transfers and the associated costs forever. Of course, these two approaches are schematic and the reality of development is far more complex. For example, there are growth patterns that are more inclusive than others and therefore less costly in terms of attaining the MDGs. Furthermore, targeted transfers and expenditures can have externalities on all aspects of social development, and can even contribute to growth.

However, poorly designed transfers and public spending can obviously be harmful to growth. The methodological objective of this study is clearly a lot more austere. It aims to evaluate the overall cost of achieving the MDGs in terms of the broad types of policies.

Figure 1.1. **Top-down *vs.* bottom-up costs by income level group**
(annual amounts)

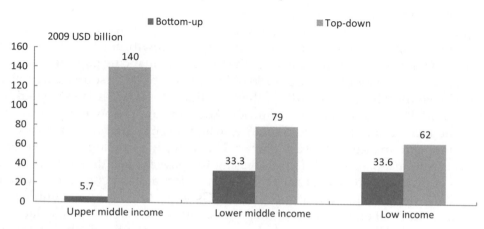

Source: Authors' calculations.

StatLink ⏧ http://dx.doi.org/10.1787/888932596023

The size of the financing gaps across regions differs considerably, as shown by Figure 1.2. According to the top-down approach, East Asia and South Asia have a minimal financing gap for achieving the MDGs in a sustainable manner. This reflects the significant progress these regions have made on MDG 1 over the past decade. In contrast, health-related needs are large in South Asia, and concentrated in a limited number of countries with a large population. Latin America and the Caribbean and sub-Saharan Africa, on the other hand, require significant additional capital to achieve enough growth to meet the MDGs on a sustainable basis.

Figure 1.2. **Top-down *vs.* bottom-up costs by region**
(annual amounts)

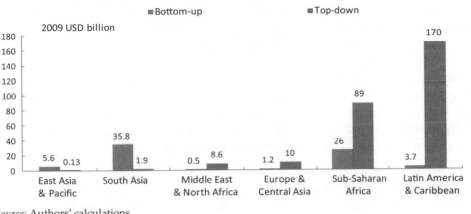

Source: Authors' calculations.

StatLink http://dx.doi.org/10.1787/888932596042

Indeed, there are developing countries where a reasonable increase in development finance will have no impact on the MDGs. For such countries, adopting a top-down approach is prohibitively expensive and makes no sense in terms of meeting the MDGs. For instance, Colombia and Venezuela have neither the largest number of poor people in the world nor even the largest share of poor people living in their countries. However, these middle-income economies are some of the most unequal and have been historically, some of the least responsive to investment and aid as captured by the long-term data over the period 1990-2015. This is why, in such cases, a bottom-up transfer and social service delivery approach is adopted.

The role of inequality cannot be overstated in explaining the large financing gaps in Latin American countries. In addition to a lack of productivity in capital investment, these countries have seen a very low reduction in poverty because high inequality has muted the impact of growth in lifting people out of poverty (Bourguignon, 2003). In the case of Colombia for instance, income inequality implies that the top-down approach needs to ensure that through growth USD 462 000 goes to the richest 10% of the population for the equivalent of USD 8 800 to go to the poorest 10% of the population because it assumes an unchanged income distribution. Consequently, reforms aimed at mitigating inequality and improving the productivity of capital investment would significantly decrease the financing gap of these countries, thereby representing a development priority.

However, in theory, reducing poverty by increasing growth is fundamentally different from, and preferable to, improving health and education by increasing spending in these areas. Similarly, there is a fundamental difference between reducing poverty by increasing growth and reducing poverty by redistributing income to the poor: once incomes improve through growth, they are much less likely to fall back significantly later, even though growth may slow down. Conversely, education, health expenditure and transfers to reduce poverty need to be maintained, or people will not remain healthy, children will not stay in school, and transfer recipients may fall back into poverty. This is why, according to our calculations, in countries where it is more affordable, the top-down approach is preferable to the bottom-up approach.

In practice, it is clear that the bottom-up approach may profitably be combined with the top-down approach and *vice versa*. An effective and progressive tax system can make the amount of financing needed to tackle poverty through growth more affordable. Conversely, growth usually makes social spending more affordable for the national Treasury. Along the same lines, given that poverty is multi-dimensional, there are often synergies between spending on education, health and the fight against extreme poverty. Capturing these kinds of effects clearly requires very in-depth data. In developing countries, such data is rarely of a sufficiently reliable quality. It also entails sophisticated modeling at the individual country level. Such analysis lies outside the scope of this study but it is being identified as research that could yield useful insights. This is one of the many reasons why the development of statistical data in developing countries is a priority.

Filling the financing gap is less costly over time in low-income countries, while achieving the Millennium goals through service delivery is eventually less costly in middle-income countries. Figure 1.3 compares the total capital cost of filling the financing gap by 2015 with the total capital cost of expenditures and transfers related to MDGs, provided they are maintained indefinitely. The total capital layout needed to fill the financing gap in low-income countries, slightly more than USD 370 billion, is slightly more than half the net present value of recurring social service expenditure related to the MDGs, USD 625 billion. In contrast, the discounted value of the recurring cash flows required to achieve the MDGs through development service delivery in middle-income countries, nearly USD 680 billion, is roughly half the financing gap in these countries, more than USD 1.3 billion.

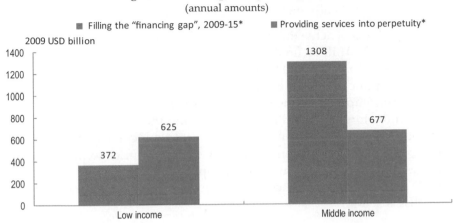

Figure 1.3. **Total capital layout required**
(annual amounts)

Notes:

*assumes filling the financing gap over the six years until 2015 with the additional assumption that the increased growth rate becomes sustainable beyond that date.

**the total expenditures needed for services here are discounted by a factor of 5.9% (the average of 6-month LIBOR in the US, 1980-2012 as documented in IMF (2011)), thus assuming that expenditure on development services continues beyond 2015.

Source: Authors' calculations.

Based on the financing gap calculations for low-income countries and by focusing on targeted transfers and expenditures for middle-income countries, attaining the first six Millennium goals worldwide is estimated to require approximately USD 120 billion.[3] Taking the same year of reference as a comparison, in 2009, ODA amounted to about USD 108 billion. However, ODA includes items that are not linked to the MDGs, such as net administrative costs, imputed student costs and debt relief. Country programmable aid refers to the sub-total of ODA that is likely to be earmarked for a particular country, with donor countries usually preparing an expenditure plan for such aid, which amounted to around USD 64 billion the same year. The incremental cost of achieving the MDGs is therefore slightly less than double the current flows of country programmable aid and also double the increase in tax revenues that is estimated in this study, which could potentially become available in developing countries. If aid flows alone had to address the cost of the MDGs and if the ratio of country programmable aid remains constant at 53%, an incremental contribution of around USD 225 billion would be required, equivalent to tripling the current amount of ODA. If humanitarian aid is considered to contribute to financing development, the increase in ODA needed would be slightly less remarkable yet politically inconceivable given current circumstances.

The total cost of achieving the first six MDGs can be split between slightly more than a USD 60 billion financing gap to be filled in 20 low-income countries and slightly less than USD 60 billion for social services linked to MDGs in 79 other low- and middle-income countries, as illustrated in Figure 1.4. This size of the financing gap for low-income countries is the amount required until 2015 to maintain the target growth rate for achieving the MDGs in a durable way. For the other low-income countries and for middle-income countries, this size is the sum of the cash transfers needed by these countries to provide enough income support to halve the number of people living on less than a dollar a-day (MDG 1) and, the sum of the cost of achieving health- and education-related goals (MDGs 2; 4-6).

Figure 1.4. **Total MDG cost estimates**
(annual amounts)

2009 USD billion

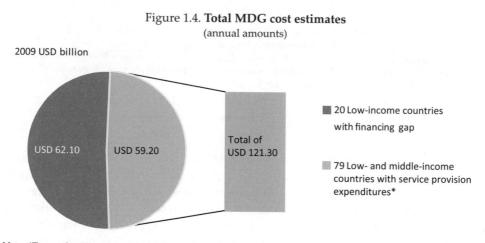

| | | |
| USD 62.10 | USD 59.20 | Total of USD 121.30 |

■ 20 Low-income countries with financing gap

■ 79 Low- and middle-income countries with service provision expenditures*

Note: *Expenditures on cash transfers, education and health.
Source: Authors' calculations.

StatLink ⫘ http://dx.doi.org/10.1787/888932596080

Notes

1. Countries with annual income per capita below roughly 1 000 USD.

2. Countries with annual income per capita below roughly 12 000 USD.

3. We only consider MDGs 1-6 which we divide into three broad categories, looking at income poverty (MDG 1), health (MDGs 4, 5, 6) and education (MDGs 2, 3). Gender equality is thus treated narrowly as an education issue because one of MDG 3's key targets is gender equality in primary education enrolment. This is admittedly unsatisfactory but it is necessary to maintain a sufficiently generalisable approach.

References

AfDB, OECD and UNECA (2010), *African Economic Outlook – Public Resource Mobilisation and Aid*, African Development Bank, Tunis and OECD, Paris.

ATISOPHON, V., J. BUEREN, G. DE PAEPE, C. GARROWAY and J.-P. STIJNS (2011), "Revisiting MDG Cost Estimates from a Domestic Resource Mobilisation Perspective", *Working Paper* No. 306, OECD Development Centre, Paris.

BOURGUIGNON, F. (2003), "The Growth Elasticity of Poverty Reduction: Explaining Heterogeneity across Countries and Time Periods", in T.S. Eicher and S.J. Turnovsky (editors) *Inequality and Growth: Theory and Policy Implications*, MIT Press, pp. 3-26.

DEVARAJAN, S., M.J. MILLER and E.V. SWANSON (2002), "Goals for Development: History, Prospects, and Costs", *Working Paper* No. 2819, World Bank, Washington, DC.

UNITED NATIONS (2001), "Report of the High-Level Panel on Financing for Development", United Nations, New York, NY.

UNDP-UNCDF (2010), *Scaling-up Support for the MDGs at the Local Level: A Global Programme Partnership Proposal*, UNDP-UNCDF, New York, NY.

WORLD BANK and IMF (2011), *Global Monitoring Report – Improving the Odds of Achieving the MDGs – Heterogeneity, Gaps and Challenges*, World Bank and International Monetary Fund, Washington, DC.

Bibliography

DOMAR, E. (1946), "Capital Expansion, Rate of Growth, and Employment", *Econometrica*, Vol. 14, No. 2, April, pp. 137-147.

EASTERLY, W. (2006a), "The Big Push Déjà Vu: A Review of Jeffrey Sach's The End of Poverty: Economic Possibilities for Our Time", *Journal of Economic Literature*, Vol. 44, Issue 1, March, pp. 96-105.

Can we still Achieve the Millennium Development Goals? © OECD 2012

EASTERLY, W. (2006b), *The White Man's Burden: Why the West's Efforts to Aid the Rest Have Done So Much Ill and So Little Good*, Penguin Press, New York, NY.

GUILLAUMONT, P. and S. GUILLAUMONT JEANNENEY (2007), "Big Push versus Absorptive Capacity: How to Reconcile the Two Approaches", *Discussion Paper* No. 2007/05, UNU-WIDER, Helsinki.

HARROD, R.F. (1939), "An Essay in Dynamic Theory", *The Economic Journal*, Vol. 49, No. 193, March, pp. 14-33.

REDDY, S. and A. HEUTY (2005), "Peer and Partner Review: A Practical Approach to Achieving the Millennium Development Goals", *Journal of Human Development and Capabilities*, Vol. 6, No. 3.

REDDY, S. and A. HEUTY (2006), "Achieving the Millennium Development Goals: What's Wrong with Existing Analytical Models?", *DESA Working Paper*, No. 30, United Nations, New York, NY.

ROSTOW, W.W. (1956), "The Take-Off into Self-Sustained Growth", *The Economic Journal*, Vol. 66, No. 261, The Royal Economic Society, pp. 25-48.

ROSTOW, W.W. (1959), "The Stages of Economic Growth", *The Economic History Review*, New Series, Vol. 12, No. 1, pp. 1-16.

UNITED NATIONS (2003), "Monterrey Consensus of the International Conference on Financing for Development", The final text of agreements and commitments adopted at the International Conference on Financing for Development, Monterrey Mexico, 18-22 March 2002, United Nations, New York, NY.

Chapter 2

The cost of measures to fight poverty and to improve health and education

Abstract

The bottom-up estimate of the global cost of targeted transfers to lift half of the world's poor out of extreme poverty (MDG 1) is nearly USD 5 billion. To achieve universal primary education (UPE - MDG 2-3), slightly less than USD 9 billion would have to be spent. On average, countries that still need to achieve UPE would need to increase spending on education by slightly more than 7%. The most challenging rate of increase in baseline expenditure is in sub-Saharan Africa, above 20%. However, it is middle-income countries that have the largest absolute expenditure shortfall, almost USD 8 billion in total. The highest costs are associated with health (MDGs 4-6) in low- and lower-middle income countries, at around USD 60 billion. In terms of regions, South Asia, and sub-Saharan Africa require the most, USD 35 billion, and USD 20 billion, respectively. The cost estimate for the promotion of gender equality and the empowerment of women (MDG 3) is partially covered by UPE (MDG 2). This study is not able to provide a cost for ensuring environmental sustainability (MDG 7). It is assumed that the global partnership for development (MDG 8) is the quintessential tool for addressing the estimated cost and not an additional cost *per se*.

Chapter 1 deals with the overall cost of achieving the MDGs. This chapter breaks down this cost by the type of MDGs related to poverty, health and education. The main objective is to identify what types of MDGs represent the most challenges in terms of financial costs and which specific types of MDGs turn out to be the most expensive to achieve within different groups of countries, both in terms of income groups and geographic regions. Therefore, this chapter focuses on the bottom-up approach because the top-down approach addresses the MDGs all together and does not allow for a breakdown by goal.

It is in low- and lower-middle countries that costs associated with achieving health-related Millennium goals are – by far – the highest. Figure 2.1 illustrates the bottom-up cost of directly reaching the MDGs through transfers and expenditure by income group. For each of these two groups of countries, achieving health-related goals in lower- and lower-middle-income countries would cost around USD 30 billion. Altogether, the costs of the health goals in these countries is around USD 60 billion, close to the USD 64 billion of country programmable aid that OECD Development Assistance Committee members already gave in 2009. In contrast, the bottom-up costs of achieving UPE are markedly weaker at slightly less than USD 9 billion in total for developing countries and slightly more than USD 1 billion – a fraction of current ODA – for low-income countries. The costs of tackling poverty through targeted transfers to the poor are under USD 5 billion. These costs are roughly the same size as those for education but concentrated in low and lower-middle income countries and split almost evenly between these two groups of countries.

Figure 2.1.**The cost of achieving poverty, health and education MDGs by income group** (annual amounts)

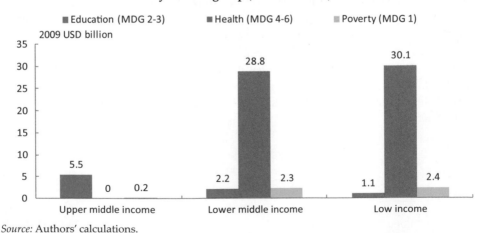

Source: Authors' calculations.

StatLink http://dx.doi.org/10.1787/888932596099

Can we still Achieve the Millennium Development Goals? © OECD 2012

Geographically, by far the highest costs are associated with achieving health goals in South Asia and sub-Saharan Africa. Figure 2.2 charts the health costs by region. In South Asia and sub-Saharan Africa, the financial costs amount to roughly USD 35 billion and USD 20 billion, respectively. Taken together, the costs of the health goals in these regions amount to roughly USD 55 billion – slightly less than the total country programmable aid allocated in 2009 (USD 64 billion). The cost of achieving UPE is smaller; about USD 1 billion in South Asia and USD 2 billion in sub-Saharan Africa. The USD 5 billion cost of combating poverty through transfers to the poor, the poverty gap approach, is largely concentrated in sub-Saharan Africa.

Figure 2.2. **The cost of achieving poverty, health and education MDGs by region**
(annual amounts)

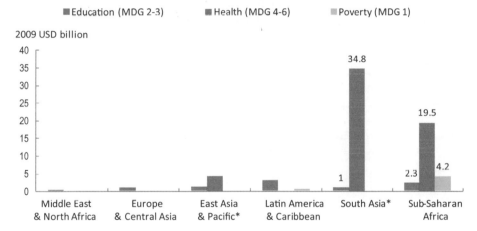

Note: *Poverty transfer is calculated for the 35 countries that are not on track to achieve MDG 1 according to financing gap calculations (East Asia & Pacific and South Asia excluded).
Source: Authors' calculations.

StatLink ᵐˢᵖ http://dx.doi.org/10.1787/888932596118

Focus on poverty

The total cost of providing transfers to the poor to lift half of them above the poverty line (MDG 1) is estimated to be slightly below USD 5 billion. Box 2.1 discusses the methodology behind these estimates. Figure 2.3 illustrates how it is distributed across income categories and regions. The greatest absolute needs are spread more or less evenly between low-income and lower-middle-income countries. Upper-middle income countries typically face much less of a poverty gap than lower and lower-middle income countries. This is in contrast with the size of their financing gap from the top-down approach discussed in Chapter 1. In countries with high levels of inequality, it is much more affordable to address poverty directly than to try and achieve enough growth in order to help the poorest members of society. The cost of halving the number of people living below the poverty line is highest in Africa and to a lesser extent, in South America.

Box 2.1. Using the poverty gap to calculate transfers to the poor (MDG 1)

The poverty gap index (Foster *et al.*, 1984) measures the mean proportionate shortfall from the poverty line for a given population. We use the poverty gap approach to measure the total transfer required to eradicate poverty in a specific country with a certain income distribution. The poverty gap is easy to calculate using the parameters of the Lorenz curve, the poverty headcount, mean income and the poverty line (Datt, 1998).

The poverty gap is a measure of the transfer that is necessary for eradicating poverty. Therefore, it is possible to compare a baseline for the poverty gap for 2015 (based on the IMF's recent forecast on prospects for the global economy by the IMF) with the poverty gap which would be expected in 2015 if MDG 1 is reached by then. The difference between these two amounts is the total annual transfer required to reduce poverty by half from its 1990 level.

Please refer to Atisophon *et al.* (2011) for further details on the methodology behind these estimates.

Figure 2.3. **Measure of targeted transfers for poverty (MDG 1) by income group and region** (annual amounts)

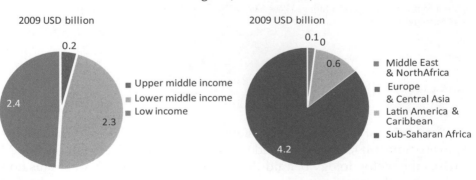

Source: Authors' calculations.

StatLink http://dx.doi.org/10.1787/888932596137

Can we still Achieve the Millennium Development Goals? © OECD 2012

The nearly USD 5 billion poverty gap estimate should be taken as a lower-bound estimate of the cost of achieving MDG 1, rather than a concrete proposal for reaching it through cash transfers. The transfers implicit in the poverty gap approach are assumed to be perfectly targeted and do not include any administrative or transaction costs. For illustrative purposes, assume that the estimated administrative cost is in the range of 10% and that the level of loss is roughly 40%. In this instance, the estimate of the financial cost of meeting MDG 1 in countries that have not yet reached this goal would have to be doubled to USD 10 billion. Besides, such calculations also assume that individual transfers should go to people who are closest to the poverty line. The transfers would therefore only go to smallest number of people necessary to ensure that the poverty headcount is halved. Although it would help reduce poverty, this type of transfer would actually exacerbate inequality. Those that are still considered to be poor after the transfers would be, on average, more deeply poor, that is much farther from the poverty line, than the poor as a group were before. Nonetheless, our estimates show that transfers to address poverty in developing countries – even after adding administrative costs – are manageable at the global level.

Focus on education

An additional USD 8.8 billion needs to be spent in 2015 to achieve universal primary education, with upper-middle-income countries having the largest expenditure shortfall, USD 5.5 billion, followed by lower-middle-income countries with USD 2.2 million. Box 2.2 discusses the methodology behind estimating the costs of achieving universal primary education and Figure 2.4 overleaf illustrates how these costs are distributed by income group and region. The region that requires the highest increase in spending compared to baseline expenditure is Latin America and Caribbean with USD 2.9 billion. This is predominantly due to the higher cost of primary education per student. Sub-Saharan Africa is the second costliest region in terms of achieving universal primary education, with an expenditure shortfall of USD 2.3 billion. The sub-Saharan Africa and the Latin American and Caribbean regions together represent close to 60% of all additional spending that would be required in 2015 to achieve universal enrolment in primary school.

Figure 2.4. **Education needs (MDGs 2-3) measures by income group and region**
(annual amounts)

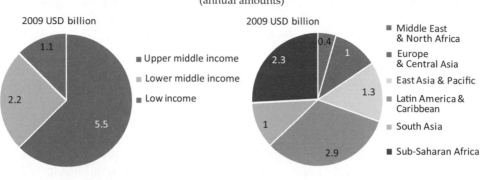

Source: Authors' calculations.

StatLink ⫘⫘ http://dx.doi.org/10.1787/888932596156

Compared to current spending and in order to reach UPE, all countries with an education expenditure shortfall would need to increase spending on education by more than 7%. Although such an increase appears to be significant, it should be achievable over time. In some respects, these estimates on the cost of UPE are arguably on the higher end. In order to be able to predict benchmark public expenditure, it is estimated that up until 2015, real public spending on primary education until 2015 will remain the same as in 2009. It is fair to assume that primary school enrolment rates will keep rising over the next few years. When other Millennium goals are pursued simultaneously, the cost of achieving UPE goes down. For instance, if poverty is also reduced significantly, the reservation wage available to children who have not completed primary schooling would play a less significant role, helping to increase net enrolment rates. Indeed, keeping children in primary education until completion is a major constraint when a family has to consider whether to make a child work or contribute to work at home.

However, the expenditure required per student tends to rise the closer a country gets to universal enrolment. For instance, providing schooling in remote areas is typically more challenging than it is in urban centres. The absolute cost of achieving UPE in Latin America and the Caribbean region is almost USD 3 billion, larger than in sub-Saharan Africa, slightly more than USD 2 billion, despite a much smaller school age population. While the Latin America and Caribbean region is closer to achieving universal primary enrolment, the cost per student is much higher in Latin American and the Caribbean than in sub-Saharan Africa. Yet, the calculations are based on the assumption that the cost per student remains constant as enrolment rates rise and they do not take account of differences in the quality of education across countries.

At the regional level, sub-Saharan Africa will require the largest increase in spending, more than 20%, in terms of the estimated amount that needs to be spent by 2015. The Middle East and North Africa comes next, with a need to increase spending by more than 8%. Within each region, substantial heterogeneity exists among countries, so much so that regional averages do not portray well how much spending has to rise in individual countries within a region. UPE may be attainable at the regional level even if it remains a far off prospect in individual countries. In some countries, the required absolute change and the necessary rate of increase in spending on education can be very high.

Box 2.2. Calculating expenditure to meet education-related goals (MDGs 2 & 3)

The cost of achieving UPE is estimated using the method proposed by Delamonica *et al.* (2001). Based on country-specific unit cost estimation of primary education, this study projected the annual additional cost of reaching a net enrolment ratio equal to 100% for primary education by 2015. According to the definition of the United Nations' Statistics Division, the net enrolment rate (NER) in primary education is the number of children of official primary school age who are enrolled in primary education as a percentage of the total number of children of the official school age population.

The NER data available for 1999-2009 and data for public expenditure on primary education come from UNESCO and the World Bank. Population census and projections are taken from the United Nations' *World Population Prospects*, 2010 revision (United Nations, Population Division). GDP per capita is taken from the IMF *World Economic Outlook* data, April 2011 edition.

Public expenditure per student (World Bank data) is the current public spending on education divided by the total number of students by level, as a percentage of GDP per capita. Public expenditure (current and capital) includes government spending on educational institutions (both public and private), education administration as well as subsidies for private entities (students/households and other private entities).

Under the baseline projection, which assumes that NERs remain constant, the projected additional expenditure can be considered an upward bound estimate of the cost that could be incurred in 2015. It is assumed that NERs will remain unchanged in order to avoid taking their progress for granted. This also prevents us from projecting an optimistic scenario when the time comes in 2015 to take stock of achievements related to education.

Please refer to Atisophon *et al.* (2011) for further details on the methodology behind these estimates.

Focus on health

Financing the Millennium health goals remains a concern for a number of countries, particularly in South Asia, which needs USD 35 billion and sub-Saharan Africa, which needs close to USD 20 billion. Box 2.3 discusses the methodology behind these estimates. Figure 2.5 shows the distribution of the financial costs of health goals by income groups and regions. Required additional spending is almost equally split between low-income countries, slightly above USD 30 billion, and lower-middle-income countries, slightly below USD 30 billion. However, in lower-middle income countries there have been significant increases in expenditure in recent years. This calls into question whether an increase in spending can be sustained. In addition, increased expenditure on health has not consistently been accompanied by improvement in health outcomes, casting doubts on the relevance of the USD 60 per capita benchmark proposed by the World Health Organization (WHO).

Results lead to the conclusion that economic growth is a major parameter for determining the cost of achieving the health MDGs, particularly if the WHO benchmark is used. The near USD 35 billion gap that South Asia must finance is concentrated in large countries such as India and Pakistan and refers to a scenario whereby spending per capita has remained unchanged between 2009 and 2015. If these economies maintain a strong growth rate after the financial crisis and the share of GDP devoted to health remains unchanged, the shortfall presented in this study will represent an overestimate of the cost of health by 2015. This said, it is also clear that beyond the evolution of the overall health budget in the countries concerned, the distribution of this expenditure remains problematic, highlighting the importance of inclusive growth for achieving the MDGs, particularly in terms of health.

Figure 2.5. **Health needs (MDGs 4-6) measures by income group and region**
(annual amounts)

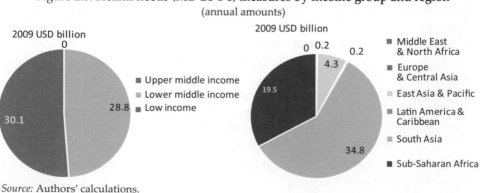

Source: Authors' calculations.

StatLink ⁐ http://dx.doi.org/10.1787/888932596175

Can we still Achieve the Millennium Development Goals? © OECD 2012

Box 2.3. **Calculating expenditure to meet health-related goals (MDGs 4, 5 & 6)**

Health-related MDGs include reducing child mortality (MDG 4), improving maternal health (MDG 5), and combating HIV/AIDS, malaria, and other epidemics (MDG 6). According to the WHO (2010), ensuring access to the types of interventions and treatments needed to address MDGs 4, 5 and 6 will require on average little more than USD 60 per capita [annually] by 2015".

It is legitimate to wonder how realistic it is to assume that USD 60 per capita would be the amount of health expenditure required to meet health-related MDGs in all developing countries. This study, however, sticks to WHO's USD 60 per capita estimate by virtue of its simplicity. With the USD 60 per capita target being maintained, to calculate how much additional expenditure will be required globally for meeting this threshold, baseline spending on health needs to be estimated under reasonable assumptions about future spending.

Current levels of government spending on health have been projected up until 2015 for 128 developing countries, where data is available. Per capita total expenditure data on health come from the WHO. IMF *World Economic Outlook* data, April 2011 edition forecasts, are used for GDP growth projections between 2011 and 2015.

These costs per inhabitant are multiplied by population projections from the United Nations' *World Population Prospects*, 2010 revision (United Nations, Population Division). Our baseline is a constant scenario, whereby initial per capita expenditure for health in 2009 remains constant. Health expenditure per capita is assumed to remain constant to avoid taking progress for granted and to project an optimistic scenario when the time comes in 2015 to take stock of achievements related to health.

Please refer to Atisophon *et al.* (2011) for further details on the methodology behind these estimates

References

Atisophon, V., J. Bueren, G. De Paepe, C. Garroway and J.-P. Stijns (2011), "Revisiting MDG Cost Estimates from a Domestic Resource Mobilisation Perspective", *Working Paper* No. 306, OECD Development Centre, Paris.

Datt, G. (1998), "Computational Tools for Poverty Measurement and Analysis", *FCND Discussion Paper* No. 50, International Food Policy Research Institute, Washington, DC.

Delamonica, E., S. Mehrotra and J. Vandemoortele (2001), "Is EFA Affordable? Estimating the Global Minimum Cost of 'Education for All'", *Innocenti Working Papers*, No. 87, UNICEF, Innocenti Research Center, Florence.

Foster, J., J. Greer and E. Thorbecke (1984), "A Class of Decomposable Poverty Measures", *Econometrica*, Vol. 52, No. 3, May 1984.

IMF (International Monetary Fund) (2011), *World Economic Outlook Data*, International Monetary Fund, Washington, DC.

United Nations (2010), *World Population Prospects*, 2010 revision, New York, NY.

WHO (2010), *The World Health Report: Health Systems Financing: The Path to Universal Coverage*, World Health Organization, Geneva.

Bibliography

Bourguignon, F., C. Diaz-Bonilla and H. Lofgren (2008), "Aid, Service Delivery, and the Millennium Development Goals in an Economy-Wide Framework", Policy Research Working Paper Series, No. 4683, World Bank, Washington, DC.

FILMER, D., J.S. HAMMER and L.H. PRICHETT (2000), "Weak Links in the Chain: A Diagnosis of Health Policy in Poor Countries", *The World Bank Research Observer*, Vol. 15, No. 2, pp. 199-224.

GLEWWE, P. and M. ZHAO (2006), "Attaining Universal Primary Schooling by 2015: An Evaluation of Cost Estimates" Chapter 7 in *Educating All Children: A Global Agenda*, J.E. Cohen, D.E. Bloom and M.B. Malin (eds), American Academy of Arts and Sciences, MIT Press, Cambridge, Masschusetts, pp. 415-454.

KLASEN, S. and S. LANGE (2011), "Getting Progress Right: Measuring Progress Towards the MDGs Against Historical Trends", *Courant Research Centre: Poverty, Equity and Growth - Discussion Papers*, No. 87, Courant Research Centre PEG.

UNESCO Institute for Statistics.

WORLD BANK data

Chapter 3

How to pay for the Millennium Development Goals?

Abstract

Upper-middle-income countries (*i.e.* countries where annual income per capita is roughly between USD 4 000 and 12 000) should be able to finance their Millennium goals themselves. Doing so would require the political will to confront income inequalities and their causes. In contrast, MDGs remain a financial major challenge for low- and lower-middle-income countries (*i.e.* countries where annual income per capita is approximately below USD 4 000). Filling at least partly these countries' financing gap through increased private capital flows is a real option. This would, however, require managing their volatility and adapting policy to optimise the social development spillovers. In the foreseeable future, it is doubtful that tax collection can make a significant contribution in the low-income countries with the largest relative needs. If the needs of the poorest citizens of the poorest countries are to be met, all the development resources – aid, private contributions, remittances, domestic taxes and private capital from traditional and emerging partners – will have a role to play. Establishing coherent policies for development will also be crucial.

The big picture

There is a stark contrast between the relative ease with which upper-middle-income countries should be able to finance their MDGs and the challenge that these goals still represent for low- and lower-middle-income countries. Figure 3.1 compares currently available development resources with the estimated needs of the different income groups. Development resources are defined here as the sum of official development assistance (ODA), foreign direct investment (FDI), migrant remittances and current tax revenues. For developing countries in all income categories, the financing gap (*i.e.* top-down costs) is larger, although in the same order of magnitude as current development financing flows, which implies that global development resources should almost double globally. While existing development resources are already in place, the financing gap, and bottom-up costs for that matter, are incremental and require additional resources.

As a corollary, policy reforms in both advanced economies and developing countries are essential to bring this financing gap down to a politically and economically achievable order of magnitude. However, the picture is not as challenging when the estimated bottom-up costs of addressing poverty, education and health through transfers and expenditure are considered instead. The bottom-up needs of lower-income and lower-middle-income countries require less than a doubling of current development financing. Increasing expenditure to meet the bottom-up costs of upper-middle-income countries only represents a small fraction of their development resources.

Figure 3.1. **Needs vs. current means**
(annual amounts)

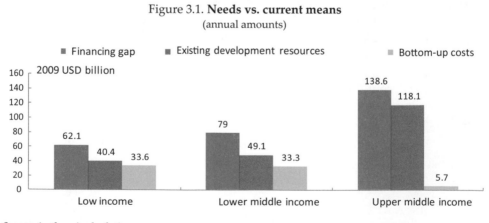

Source: Authors' calculations.

StatLink ⏳ http://dx.doi.org/10.1787/888932596194

ODA and (gross) private capital flows from Development Assistance Committee (DAC) member countries to developing countries have grown considerably over the last four decades and particularly the last ten years. Figure 3.2 plots ODA and private capital flows in real terms since 1970. The upturn in private capital flows to development partners compared with official development flows over the last 40 years is considerable. Grants by private voluntary organisations have also grown although, at USD 22 billion, they are still in a smaller order of magnitude than ODA and private capital.

Figure 3.2. **Concessionary and private capital flows from DAC member countries to developing countries, 1970-2009**

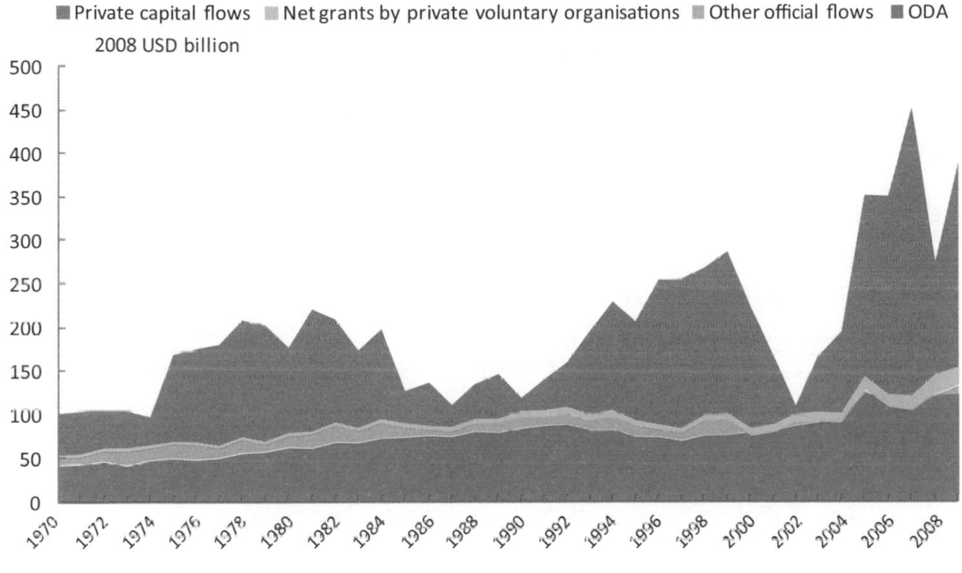

■ Private capital flows ■ Net grants by private voluntary organisations ■ Other official flows ■ ODA

Note: Net other official flows (OOFs) were negative in 2000-01, 2004 and 2006-07.
Source: Authors' calculations based on OECD-DAC.

StatLink ᘓᶴ http://dx.doi.org/10.1787/888932596213

The order of magnitude and growth of private capital flows are such that the prospect of their at least partly filling the financing gap in low-income countries is a real option. But the very high volatility of these flows is equally notable. Should private capital comprise an even larger share of development resources, its volatility would have to be properly managed so that it does not exacerbate macroeconomic instability in developing countries. These flows peaked in 2007 at above USD 330 billion, only to sink below USD 130 billion in

2008 – just under their 1978 level in real terms. The latest available data does not yet indicate a recovery of private capital flows to developing countries since the start of the global crisis.

While aid flows doubled between 2000 and 2010 in nominal dollar terms, this scaling up has been less sizable when considered as a share of the GDP of DAC member countries. Figure 3.3 contrasts official development assistance and private capital flows until 2010 as a percentage of the total GDP of DAC member countries. The fact that official development assistance still falls short of the 0.7% of GDP target for DAC countries highlights the need for the latter to deliver on commitments made in Monterrey (2002), Gleneagles (2005), Accra (2008) and most recently Busan (2011). Fulfilling the substantial commitments the DAC countries have made since the 2000 Millennium Declaration is a key criterion for reaching MDG 8 – building a global partnership for development. Further, the order of magnitude of the financing gap underlines that it is crucial for DAC member countries to abide by their commitment to deliver more effective aid and improve the coherence of their policies for development.

Figure 3.3. Official development assistance and private capital flows from DAC member countries to developing countries, 1970-2010

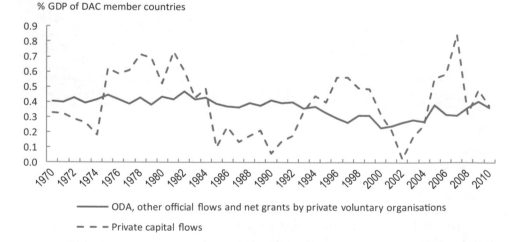

% GDP of DAC member countries

——— ODA, other official flows and net grants by private voluntary organisations

– – – Private capital flows

Source: Authors' calculations based on OECD-DAC.

StatLink ⬛ᵢₛ🏴 http://dx.doi.org/10.1787/888932596232

Focus on ODA

The symbolic weight given the oft-quoted goal of increasing official development assistance to 0.7% of GDP for DAC members needs to be re-examined. This 0.7% target, which is often used as a measure of progress on MDG 8, actually derives from back-of-the-envelope calculations by economists Jan Tinbergen and Hollis Chenery in the context of the first "Decade of Development" in the 1960s. They estimated that total capital flows to the developing world should amount to about 1% of the developed world's Gross National Income, or GNI (Clemens and Moss, 2005; Vandemoortele, 2011). At the time, private capital flows to developing countries constituted approximately 0.3% of developed countries' GNI; therefore, they considered that governments could provide the remaining 0.7%. In fact, in the 1970s, late 1990s and mid-2000s, private capital flows from DAC members were significantly higher than 0.3% of GNI. As Figure 3.3 shows, these flows also exceeded the share of DAC countries' production transferred to development partners as ODA. On the other hand, given the experienced unpredictable crises that have shaken the world economy since the 1960s, volatile private capital flows could actually imply development finance needs exceeding 1% of the GNI of OECD countries. Indeed, every crisis jeopardises some of the social progress achieved by developing countries (see, for instance, the 2011 edition of the *Report on Millennium Development Goals*, UNDP, 2011).

In any case, budgetary pressures on many DAC member countries are now such that expecting official assistance to remain constant in nominal terms is already optimistic. Further, the Accra Agenda for Action (2008) strongly emphasises ownership of development policies and domestic resource mobilisation. Moreover, aid flows might dissuade the governments of recipient countries from mobilising domestic resources (including through tax collection), thus maintaining their dependence on aid and absolving them of their obligation to be accountable to taxpayers. It is therefore necessary to look beyond increased ODA as a pre-existing condition to reach the MDGs and to assess instead potential alternative sources of financing in developing countries in general and low-income countries in particular. Indeed, the Busan Partnership for Effective Development Co-operation (Busan, 2011) calls for facilitating a broad spectrum of funding sources including domestic resource mobilisation and recognises the need for new financial instruments and co-operation modalities (paragraph 10 of the Declaration).

Focus on private capital flows

If private capital is to play a larger role in development, governments must do more to encourage its flows and manage their volatility. Private capital is drawn to economic returns. It is therefore sensitive to economic policies in recipient countries. Yet economic returns are also sensitive to external conditions, such as commodity price fluctuations and other factors beyond the control of recipient countries. The rising share of capital flows from emerging partners to developing countries has gone hand in hand with a shift in the kinds of projects being financed. Traditional donors tend to fund social infrastructure projects, such as water and roads, of particular relevance to the Millennium goals. By contrast, the 2011 edition of the *African Economic Outlook* (AfDB, OECD and UNECA, 2011) documented that emerging partners tend to focus on production infrastructure, such as energy and railways. While investing in a country's production capacity is likely to contribute to growth, it may not always directly help reach the MDGs. Countries dealing with emerging partners must therefore provide in their national development plans for mechanisms allowing foreign direct investment to generate inclusive growth and job creation, and boosting development results. Thus it is important to cooperate at the regional level to prevent the partners of African countries to pitch them in tax competition in a bid to attract foreign investment (see again AfDB, OECD and UNECA, 2011). Improving policies governing migrant remittances, including those linked to the bond market, to ensure that these funds contribute more systematically to investment would also be helpful.

However, assuming that private capital can play a comparable role to make up for financing gaps, in many low-income countries it cannot yet be considered a realistic substitute for official financing. Given the pressure on ODA budgets, the growing focus on financing Millennium goals with private capital will pose new challenges for countries engaged in that effort. Private capital is a largely untapped source of MDG financing, but this does not entail necessarily that governments should borrow on non-concessional terms to achieve their goals. While borrowing may be acceptable in some situations, indebtedness remains problematic, especially for fragile states or countries with a weak administrative framework. Indeed, concerns about institutional quality and absorption capacity also apply to non-concessional forms of financing the MDGs, notably through private capital flows. A rising dominance of private capital flows is expected and this expectation highlights how important it is for many countries to build up an institutional framework guaranteeing the medium-term sustainability of their public finances.

Focus on domestic resource mobilisation

In upper-middle-income countries and much of Latin America, poverty should decline significantly if progressive fiscal policies are applied. The 2009 and 2011 editions of the *Latin American Economic Outlook* (OECD, 2008; OECD and ECLAC, 2012) showed that taxes and public expenditures have had very little impact on reducing social inequality in many Latin American countries. In many developing countries, fiscal policy does not play a progressive role and can even hinder individuals and small enterprises (see, for instance, the 2010 edition of the *African Economic Outlook* (AfDB, OECD and UNECA, 2010). Figure 3.4 shows estimated potential tax revenue increases by region.

Figure 3.4. **Total potential tax increase by region**
(annual amounts)

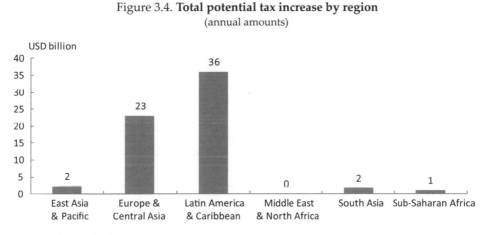

Source: Authors' calculations.

StatLink ⬛⬛ http://dx.doi.org/10.1787/888932596251

Some countries, including those with significant financing gaps, can realise sizable gains in tax revenue. According to tax effort measures, Colombia, Guatemala and Paraguay could raise several billion dollars by improving tax collection, and Democratic Republic of the Congo (DRC) could also raise a substantial sum. Figure 3.5 shows the amount of domestic resources that developing countries could raise through increased tax revenue as representing about half of the USD 120 billion in extra annual resources required to reach the MDGs by 2015. Figure 3.5 also shows the tremendous discrepancy in potential tax revenue between low-income and lower-middle-income countries on the one hand, and upper-middle-income countries on the other hand.

Figure 3.5. **Total potential tax increase by income group and average as a share of GDP**
(annual amounts)

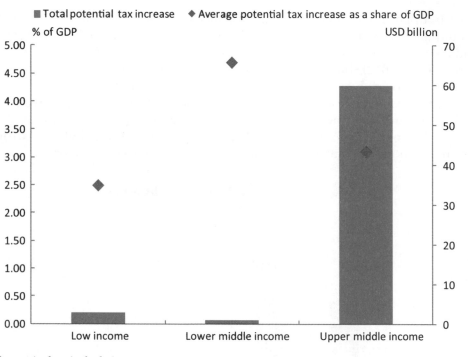

Source: Authors' calculations.

StatLink ⫘ http://dx.doi.org/10.1787/888932596270

However, it is doubtful that domestic resource mobilisation can contribute significantly to filling the financing gap of low- and lower-middle-income countries, which proportionally have the largest needs. Tax effort calculations for countries with a financing gap and for which tax revenue data is available show that over half already collect more taxes than would be expected given their characteristics. While potential additional resources as a share of GDP are similar across income groups, the absolute potential amounts of additional tax differ greatly. Thus, it is not surprising that the scale of additional tax revenue available in upper-middle-income countries can – supposing the political will to reduce income inequalities – cover the cost of MDG-related services calculated in the previous sections. The sames does not apply to low-income countries, which could never cover the costs of MDG-related transfers and public expenditure or their financing gap in this manner.

A detailed look at fiscal policies in individual countries could uncover additional means to raise tax revenue. Further, international tax co-operation efforts should, in principle, bear fruit in developing countries by helping them control illicit flows and combat tax evasion. However, as the deadline for the Millennium goals is 2015, it should be noted that raising additional revenue takes time and can constitute a challenge in low-income countries with limited administrative capacity. Bold efforts would be required to overcome these difficulties in such a short time, especially given the capacity constraints and governance issues. For instance, if improved tax collection focuses too much on natural resource revenues, a potential reversal in commodity prices could hinder revenue mobilisation and progress towards the Millennium goals.

In short, enhanced tax collection is not a panacea for financing development, insofar as many countries that could collect additional revenue are already well on their way to achieving the MDGs. There is a mismatch between the countries that could mobilise additional domestic resources and those that actually need financing to meet the MDGs. While it is estimated that middle-income countries need half of the financing, most of the USD 64 billion in potential domestic resource increase (through heightened tax revenues) is concentrated in middle-income countries that are not lagging on MDG progress.

This mismatch raises the question of whether, and to what extent, some emerging countries are in a position to both increase tax revenue and scale up their own contributions to development co-operation and investment in other countries. Discussions at the Fourth High-Level Forum on Aid Effectiveness in Busan, Korea, highlighted the unique and growing importance of South-South co-operation. Hence, it is interesting to consider how increased domestic resources in some developing countries could help other developing countries. While it may be tempting to compare these flows to official development assistance from traditional partners, the Busan discussions underscored the fact that the principles, commitments and actions agreed among traditional development partners only apply to South-South partners on a voluntary basis.

Box 3.1. **Estimating the scope for scaling-up domestic
resources mobilisation**

The degree to which countries can scale up their own domestic resource mobilisation to finance the Millennium goals is explained by adopting the techniques used by Piancastelli (2001) and Bird *et al.* (2004; 2008) to calculate "tax effort" in developing countries. The tax effort index compares projected tax revenue to actual tax revenue and estimates the additional tax revenue that could be collected if a country improved tax collection. Empirically, taxes as a share of GDP depend on a country's level of development, the share of the economy that is formal or industrialised and its openness to trade. Generally, higher levels of development and openness coincide with higher levels of tax collection.

Tax revenue is projected using a regression model for the period 2000-10 for all countries for which data for tax revenue, agricultural share, trade openness and GDP per capita were available. The ratio of predicted tax revenues to actual tax revenues is called "tax effort":

$$Tax\ effort = \frac{Predicted\ tax\ revenue\ as\ a\ share\ of\ GDP}{Actual\ tax\ revenue\ as\ a\ share\ of\ GDP}$$

Countries with a tax effort below 1 are collecting fewer taxes than they would be expected to given their structural characteristics, while countries with a tax effort above 1 are collecting more taxes than expected.

The reader is referred to Atisophon *et al.* (2011) for further details on the methodology behind these estimates.

Putting it all together

Overall, upper-middle-income countries should be able to mobilise enough domestic financing to meet the MDGs. This presupposes the political will to tackle income equality and follow a bottom-up approach using targeted transfers and expenditure to address poverty, education and health. Figure 3.6 contrasts development resources with financing needs and bottom-up costs by country income group. While the additional tax potential of the upper-middle-income countries falls short of meeting their financing gap, it is clearly larger than the bottom-up costs of addressing poverty, education and health through transfers and expenditure. Whether this is true in practice for each upper-middle-income country is a separate empirical question that requires detailed country-level investigations both of MDG costs and actual tax potential. Moreover, fiscal space can also be expanded by improving the quality and progressiveness of public spending; reforms in this area would help reduce the cost of MDGs in upper-middle-income countries.

Figure 3.6. **Current and potential development finance by income group**
(annual amounts)

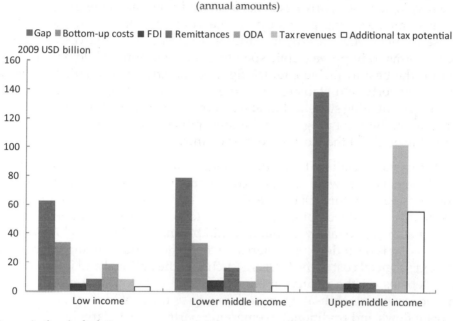

Source: Authors' calculations.

StatLink ⟶ http://dx.doi.org/10.1787/888932596289

Conversely, neither low-income nor lower middle-income countries can be expected to mobilise enough domestic resources to meet the poverty, education and health-related costs of the Millennium goals, even when applying a bottom-up approach to development services. Not only does the additional tax potential of low-income and lower-middle-income countries fall short of meeting their financing gap in a top-down approach, it is also insufficient to cover the bottom-up costs of addressing poverty, education and health through transfers and expenditure. Detailed country-level analyses would probably reveal exceptions and additional tax capacity not captured in these estimates. But the country group averages also hide considerably more challenging situations in terms of raising development resources than Figure 3.6 suggests.

Policy options to meet MDG needs in low- and lower-middle-income countries should not be of the "either-or" type, but rather of the "this-and-that" type. The situation depicted in Figure 3.6 implies that domestic resource mobilisation in low-income and lower-middle-income countries can only comprise one element among the array of possible development resources to be mobilised for development. Official development assistance, co-operation with emerging partners, private capital from traditional and emerging partners, migrant remittances and grants by private voluntary organisations must all increase to meet MDG needs, in addition to domestic resources and other policy reforms to improve public spending. Furthermore, while our study is based on the best available country figures, the strong correlation between economic poverty and statistical weakness must be acknowledged – which entails that combating statistical weakness is not only urgent, but also necessary and profitable. Short of progress in this area, policy makers will remain largely blind to the plight of the world's poorest countries.

At this stage, a failure to achieve synergies amongst the broad community of development actors would result in condemning these populations to poverty for the foreseeable future. Of course, the precise mix of development resources best suited to each developing country should be the object of intense debate – starting at the national level – but it would be unadvisable to exclude *a priori* any particular type of development resource. In the present circumstances, the estimated financial cost of the MDGs is such that the national and international policy debates on the relative merits of official development assistance *vs* domestic resource mobilisation, concessionary *vs* for-profit investment, public *vs* private flows and traditional *vs* emerging partners seem largely misplaced. If the needs of the poorest citizens of the poorest countries are to be met, all development resources will need to be mobilised, exploiting all possible synergies. Improved domestic and international policies should play a key role in boosting the social impact of all available resources, whatever their volume.

References

Accra Agenda for Action (2008).

AfDB, OECD and UNECA (2010), *African Economic Outlook – Public Resource Mobilisation and Aid,* African Development Bank, Tunis and OECD, Paris.

AfDB, OECD and UNECA (2011), *African Economic Outlook : Africa and its Emerging Partners,* African Development Bank, Tunis and OECD, Paris.

Atisophon, V., J. Bueren, G. De Paepe, C. Garroway and J.-P. Stijns (2011), "Revisiting MDG Cost Estimates from a Domestic Resource Mobilisation Perspective", *Working Paper* No. 306, OECD Development Centre, Paris.

Bird, R.M., J. Martinez-Vazquez and B. Torgler (2004), "Societal Institutions and Tax Effort in Developing Countries", *International Studies Program Working Paper Series,* No. 0406, International Studies Program, Andrew Young School of Policy Studies, Georgia State University.

Bird, R.M., J. Martinez-Vazquez and B. Torgler (2008), "Tax Effort in Developing Countries and High Income Countries: The Impact of Corruption, Voice and Accountability", *Economic Analysis and Policy* (EAP), Queensland University of Technology (QUT), School of Economics and Finance, Vol. 38(1), March, pp. 55-71.

Busan (2011), Fourth High Level Forum on Aid Effectiveness, 29 November-1 December 2011, Busan Partnership for Effective Development Co-operation, Busan, Korea.

Clemens, M.A. and T.J. Moss (2005), "Ghost of 0.7%: Origins and Relevance of the International Aid Target", Working Paper 68, Center for Global Development, Washington, DC.

Gleneagles (2005), The 31st G-8 Summit, 6-8 July 2005, Scotland, United Kingdom

OECD (2008), *Latin American Economic Outlook 2009,* OCDE, Paris.

OECD and ECLAC (2012), *Latin American Economic Outlook 2012: Transforming the State for Development,* OECD, Paris.

Piancastelli, M. (2001), "Measuring the Tax Effort of Developed and Developing Countries: Cross Country Panel Data Analysis - 1985/95", *Institute of Applied Economic Research Working Papers No. 818.*

UNITED NATIONS (2003), "Monterrey Consensus of the International Conference on Financing for Development", The final text of agreements and commitments adopted at the International Conference on Financing for Development, Monterrey Mexico, 18-22 March 2002, United Nations, New York, NY.

UNDP (2011), *Millennium Development Goals Report*, UNDP, New York, NY.

VANDEMOORTELE, J. (2011), "The MDG Story: Intention Denied", *Development and Change*, Vol. 42, Issue 1, pp. 1-21.

Bibliography

CHENERY, H.B. and A.M. STROUT (1966), "Foreign Assistance and Economic Development", *The American Economic Review*, Vol. LVI, No. 4, Part I.

CLEMENS, M.A., C.J. KENNY and T.J. Moss. (2007), "The Trouble with the MDGs: Confronting Expectations of Aid and Development Success", **World Development**, Vol. 35, No. 5, pp. 735-751, 2007.

VANDEMOORTELE, J. and R. ROY (2005), "Making Sense of MDG Costing", in F. Cheru and C. Bradford (eds.), *The Millennium Development Goals: Raising the Resources to Tackle World Poverty*, Zed Books, London.

Chapter 4

What strategies to achieve the Millennium Development Goals?

Abstract

Upper-middle-income countries (annual income per capita just above above USD 4 000) should succeed in meeting the MDGs using their domestic resources, through targeted cash transfers and expenditure programmes addressing poverty, education and health. In low-income and lower-middle-income countries (annual income per capita roughly below USD 4 000), it is important to pursue institutional reforms to enhance tax collection in order to ensure adequate financing for the MDGs. In low-income countries (annual income per capita below approximately USD 1 000), the incremental cost of meeting the Millennium goals is close to country programmable aid currently being spent globally. Now more than ever, private voluntary donations, co-operation mechanisms with emerging countries, migrant remittances and private capital flows will be required to complement aid. In developing countries, the challenge is twofold: first, to adapt national development strategies to ensure that these various flows contribute to inclusive growth, job creation and social development; second, to implement reforms to improve the quality of public expenditure. As for advanced economies, they are now obligated to improve aid effectiveness and to adopt policies that are more coherent for development.

The estimated USD 120 billion required to achieve the Millennium Development Goals is affordable at the global level, provided countries undertake the necessary reforms and adopt a broad view of the resources that can bring results in countries lagging behind in reaching the goals. Official development assistance (ODA) remains an essential source of financing for MDG achievement, particularly in low-income countries. OECD DAC member countries must therefore deliver on their commitments – particularly to establish policies more coherent for development and make aid more effective – to set in motion a successful development process. Domestic resource mobilisation through increased tax revenue seems the most sustainable and dependable means of funding the Millennium goals. While this observation is particularly valid in upper-middle-income countries over the shorter term; it extends to all developing countries in the longer term. Developing countries have made notable efforts to improve tax collection, which are beginning to bear fruit. However, much remains to be done to improve the quality of public expenditure.

Private capital flows have grown and are now on a par with ODA, with the potential to play an even stronger role. These flows peaked in 2007 at above USD 330 billion, but sank below USD 130 billion in 2008. More should be done to address their high volatility to avoid exacerbating macroeconomic instability in recipient countries. National development strategies must be adapted to ensure that private capital flows – whether from traditional DAC donor countries or emerging countries – are fully exploited to promote the Millennium goals. Policies governing migrant remittances should also ensure that they contribute more systematically to investment, *e.g.* by developing the bond market. Grants by private voluntary organisations have also increased although, at around USD 20 billion, they are in a smaller order of magnitude than ODA and private capital.

How much does it cost?

This study estimates the cost of achieving the first six Millennium goals at a little over USD 120 billion of new resources beyond the current flows of investment, ODA and public spending in the developing world. This amount is larger than earlier estimates. This study aims to question the traditional aid-centric view of the MDGs. Countries actually have a wide range of policy options to reach their development goals. While some may have more leeway than others in formulating a development strategy, they all share the need to allocate limited political capital and prioritise reform efforts.

The financial cost of the MDGs in upper-middle-income countries, in Latin America for instance, often stems less from from population poverty in absolute terms than from high inequality or market structures that are responsible for below-average capital productivity and savings. In these countries, solving poverty by stimulating growth through development finance is an expensive exercise. However, given political will to address income inequalities, enhance tax collection and improve the quality of public expenditure, they have the potential to reach the goals through targeted transfers to the poor and spending on education and health. Policy reforms to boost growth and make it more inclusive would lower the cost of the MDGs in these countries.

Conversely, financing development through domestic growth or targeted transfers and spending is unaffordable for most low-income countries and some lower-middle-income countries, where ODA will remain a key complement to domestic fiscal revenues for the foreseeable future. For these countries, the most cost-effective option is for all development partners to go for a "big push", *i.e.* financing growth in low-income countries so they can meet the MDGs durably, rather than continuing to finance transfers and expenditures year after year. This should not, however, understate the potential of direct mechanisms for alleviating poverty and funding universal primary education and health-related MDGs. In low-income countries, even a relatively small increase in spending towards these goals, provided it is designed to be effective, could go a very long way. In these countries, universal education – a goal with important spillover effects on gender equality – would only cost slightly over USD 1 billion. This is a fraction of some of the figures discussed in the national policy debates in OECD countries since the onset of the financial crisis.

Who pays?

Additional external resources are undoubtedly needed. While aid flows have essentially doubled between 2000 and 2010 in nominal dollars terms, this increase has been less significant as a percentage of the GDP of DAC member countries. Hence, it is still essential for these countries to make good on their commitments, particularly with regard to aid effectiveness of the coherence of policies for development. Low-income countries receive about 65% of total ODA. As these have the most need for external development resources, consideration should be given to focusing on them any increase in ODA. Indeed, many recipient countries do not bear the highest MDG financing costs.

Domestic resource mobilisation, particularly more effective tax collection, also plays an important role in the development finance toolbox. For instance, as noted in the 2010 edition of the *African Economic Outlook* (AfDB, OECD and UNECA; 2010), tax revenue is approximately ten times higher than ODA in Africa. More effective tax collection in developing countries could yield over half of the amount needed to meet the MDGs – in other words, over USD 60 billion. If the political will is there, middle-income countries – and particularly upper-middle-income countries, where the annual income exceeds USD 4 000 per capita – should be able to meet the MDGs thanks to their domestic resources, using targeted cash transfer and expenditure programmes targeting poverty, education and health, especially if they undertake the necessary reforms to improve the quality of public spending.

That said, the increase in domestic resource mobilisation should not serve as a pretext to exempt donor countries from honouring their commitments. In any case, one can only depend so much on domestic resource mobilisation. Among the countries that require additional resources to halve their poverty rates (MDG 1), more than half are already collecting more taxes than could be expected given their structural characteristics. Conversely, many of the countries with scope to improve revenue collection are already well on the way to achieving the MDGs. This raises the question of whether, and to what extent, some emerging countries could both increase their tax revenues and scale up their own contributions to development co-operation and investment in other developing countries.

While providing an important complement to traditional financing sources, improved tax collection is not a panacea for development funding. In low-income countries, institutional reforms take years to bear fruit, even if properly prioritised, implemented and supported at the international level. Moreover, in developing countries, it is important to ensure that taxation does not exacerbate inequalities and that a fair tax system emphasises controlling illicit flows and combating corporate tax evasion – particularly by multinational companies and the mining sector. This underlines how important it is to further good governance at all levels: to start with, in development aid, but also in developing countries' tax administration and mining sector and, last but not least, in central and local governments' social sectors. This is a long-term task that requires considerable international co-ordination but the key is maximum transparency in all financial transactions, as well as improving accounting standards and budgetary practices.

Mechanically concluding from this study's MDG cost estimates that the main solution to the MDG challenges is a quantitative increase in development finance – whether foreign or domestic – is another pitfall. MDG cost estimates are contingent on the quality of policy, public spending and ODA. Thus, the order of magnitude of cost estimates argues for improving aid effectiveness and designing policies that are more coherent for development in OECD countries. It also highlights the importance of political reforms to improve the quality of public spending, enhance investment productivity and generate more inclusive, employment-intensive growth in developing countries.

The political reality is that in a context where the most optimistic scenario is for ODA to remain constant, aid will need to be complemented by policy reforms in both developing and OECD countries as well as by the entire range of development resources – private voluntary donations, co-operation mechanisms with emerging countries, migrant remittances and private capital flows. The challenge will be to create a global partnership that will fully exploit flow synergies, ensuring that they contribute to inclusive and job-intensive growth and social development.

What about the MDGs beyond 2015?

What's next? Do the relatively high costs of financing the MDGs offer any guidance on how international development goals will be pursued after 2015? Clearly, many of the goals will need attention beyond that date – would it be sensible to simply push back the deadline? Furthermore, what kind of benchmarks should those countries that have achieved the MDGs set to refocus development efforts beyond 2015? Is development "achieved" once a country has reduced extreme poverty by half? What is the right balance between nationally relevant and internationally comparable goals?

Should the focus be on aid effectiveness and capacity building? Should it be on institutions, capacity and citizen approaches? Should a regional approach be taken? If so, referring to income categories, such as low- and middle-income countries – or should the approach be modulated to account for fragile countries, for instance? Should a sectoral approach be taken, possibly focusing on agriculture as a means to solve hunger and unemployment? Should reforms focus instead on job creation, or improving the quality of public expenditure? Should an environment that promotes growth be favoured, or growth that is respectful of the environment, and thus of sustainable development goals? Should inequalities be tackled?

Paradoxically, this emphasis on putting each country in charge of its destiny and building its own development strategy is consistent with interpreting global MDG targets as national policy goals. For want of more effective international co-ordination on how to achieve the Millennium goals, individual countries have been forced to identify and deploy their own implementation capacity. While this situation may stigmatise or handicap those countries that initially faced the highest obstacles, can it be argued that it also empowers national administrations and governments to take ownership of their development agenda?

References

AfDB, OECD and UNECA (2010), *African Economic Outlook – Public Resource Mobilisation and Aid*, African Development Bank, Tunis and OECD, Paris.

Bibliography

OECD (2011), *Perspectives on Global Development 2012: Social Cohesion in a Shifting World*, OECD, Paris.

REDDY, S. and A. HEUTY (2008), "Global Development Goals: The Folly of Technocratic Pretensions", *Development Policy Review*, Vol. 26, No. 1, pp. 5-28.

ROSENSTEIN-RODAN, P. N. (1943) "Problems of Industrialisation of Eastern and South-Eastern Europe", *The Economic Journal*, Vol. 53, No. 210/211 (Jun.-Sep., 1943), pp. 202-211.

UNITED NATIONS (2009), "Doha Declaration on Financing for Development", (A/CONF.212/L.1/Rev.1*), United Nations, New York, NY.

ORGANISATION FOR ECONOMIC CO-OPERATION AND DEVELOPMENT

The OECD is a unique forum where governments work together to address the economic, social and environmental challenges of globalisation. The OECD is also at the forefront of efforts to understand and to help governments respond to new developments and concerns, such as corporate governance, the information economy and the challenges of an ageing population. The Organisation provides a setting where governments can compare policy experiences, seek answers to common problems, identify good practice and work to co-ordinate domestic and international policies.

The OECD member countries are: Australia, Austria, Belgium, Canada, Chile, the Czech Republic, Denmark, Estonia, Finland, France, Germany, Greece, Hungary, Iceland, Ireland, Israel, Italy, Japan, Korea, Luxembourg, Mexico, the Netherlands, New Zealand, Norway, Poland, Portugal, the Slovak Republic, Slovenia, Spain, Sweden, Switzerland, Turkey, the United Kingdom and the United States. The European Union takes part in the work of the OECD.

OECD Publishing disseminates widely the results of the Organisation's statistics gathering and research on economic, social and environmental issues, as well as the conventions, guidelines and standards agreed by its members.

OECD DEVELOPMENT CENTRE

The Development Centre of the Organisation for Economic Co-operation and Development was established by decision of the OECD Council on 23 October 1962 and comprises 24 member countries of the OECD: Austria, Belgium, Chile, the Czech Republic, Finland, France, Germany, Iceland, Ireland, Israel, Italy, Korea, Luxembourg, Mexico, the Netherlands, Norway, Poland, Portugal, Slovak Republic, Spain, Sweden, Switzerland, Turkey and the United Kingdom. In addition, the following non-OECD countries are members of the Development Centre: Brazil (since March 1994); India (February 2001); Romania (October 2004); Thailand (March 2005); South Africa (May 2006); Egypt and Viet Nam (March 2008); Colombia (July 2008); Indonesia (February 2009); Costa Rica, Mauritius, Morocco and Peru (March 2009), the Dominican Republic (November 2009), Senegal (February 2011), and Argentina and Cape Verde (March 2011). The Commission of the European Communities also takes part in the Centre's Governing Board.

The Development Centre, whose membership is open to both OECD and non-OECD countries, occupies a unique place within the OECD and in the international community. Members finance the Centre and serve on its Governing Board, which sets the biennial work programme and oversees its implementation.

The Centre links OECD members with developing and emerging economies and fosters debate and discussion to seek creative policy solutions to emerging global issues and development challenges. Participants in Centre events are invited in their personal capacity.

A small core of staff works with experts and institutions from the OECD and partner countries to fulfil the Centre's work programme. The results are discussed in informal expert and policy dialogue meetings, and are published in a range of high-quality products for the research and policy communities. The Centre's Study Series presents in-depth analyses of major development issues. Policy Briefs and Policy Insights summarise major conclusions for policy makers; Working Papers deal with the more technical aspects of the Centre's work.

For an overview of the Centre's activities, please see *www.oecd.org/dev.*

OECD PUBLISHING, 2, rue André-Pascal, 75775 PARIS CEDEX 16
(41 2012 01 1 P) ISBN 978-92-64-17323-1– No. 59933 2012-05

NOTES